THE
PILGRIMAGE

5

**Five Muslims make
the great discovery**

PENFOLD BOOKS

Contents

Introduction

Each year up to two million Muslims make their Hajj (Pilgrimage) to Mecca and Medina. It qualifies as the world's largest international gathering. As thousands spill into the arena that surrounds the Ka'aba, the Black Rock at Mecca, many lift their hands to receive spiritual energy from the Rock. Adorned in white robes, the Hajjis swarm around this sacred site where it all began with Muhammad in the 7th Century AD. They have reached the heartland of Islam.

The Hajj to Mecca reminds us of the spiritual journey in which all human beings are engaged. In this booklet 5 Muslims recall their own personal pilgrimage. From Egypt, Iran, Pakistan, Saudi Arabia, Israel and India, Sunnis and Shi'ites have come together to relate their amazing life stories.

Intifada

By Walid
From Bethlehem, Israel

My birth took place in Bethlehem, Israel, on one of the holiest days of Islam - the birthday of the Muslim prophet Muhammad. My father, a Palestinian Muslim, taught English and Islamic studies in the Holy Land. He married an American woman during his studies in the United States in 1956. Fearing the likely negative impact of the American way of life on our family, my parents left the USA in 1960 to live in Bethlehem. A change of job brought my family to Saudi Arabia, then back to the Holy Land, this time to the lowest place on earth, Jericho.

I shall never forget the first song I learned in school entitled, *"Arabs our beloved and Jews our dogs."* I repeated the words without even knowing the meaning of the word 'Jew'! As I grew up in the Holy Land I lived through several battles between the Arabs and the Jews. The Six Day War, which took place while I lived in Jericho, resulted, among other things, in the capture of old Jerusalem by the Jews. This brought great disappointment to all my fellow Arabs and Muslims around the world.

During the war, the American Council in Jerusalem offered my family evacuation assistance, but my father refused because he loved his country. How I remember that war. The noise of the bombing and shelling that continued day and night for six days; the looting of shops and houses by the Arabs in Jericho, and the many who fled East in fear to cross the Jordan River. On the seventh day a Rabbi by the name of Goren blew a ram's horn on the Wailing Wall in Jerusalem declaring

4

the victory. Many Jews claimed it represented a parallel with Joshua from ancient history, who conquered Jericho after encircling the city. To my father in Jericho, it seemed like the end of the world. During the war he used to listen to Jordanian radio. He reassured us, from what he heard, that the Arabs were winning – but in the end it turned out to have been mere propaganda.

When we moved back to Bethlehem, my father enrolled us in an Anglican-Lutheran school, since they had a particularly good English course. My brother, my sister and I felt isolated as the only Muslims in the school. Being half American, when the teachers would beat us, the other students simply laughed. When the Bible class started, I always left the room and stayed outside. One day, I walked into the Bible class and the class bully shouted, *"We don't want this half-American half-Muslim in here!"* I refused to leave, so the teacher requested me to sit down. That act changed the school's policy and from then on the school allowed Muslims to study the Bible – something I did for the next three years.

My father then transferred me to the Government school where the teachers instructed me in the way of Islam. Among other things, I learned that one day, in fulfilment of an ancient prophecy by Muhammad, a battle would rage, resulting in the capture of the Holy Land and the slaughter of all the Jews. The prophecy is from Muhammad's Book of Traditions:

"The day of judgment shall not come to pass until a tribe of Muslims defeat a tribe of Jews." (Narrated by Abu Hurairah, Sahih Muslim, Hadith #6985; Sahih al-Bukhari, Vol. 4, #177)

When Muhammad was asked where this would take place, he said: *"In Jerusalem and the surrounding nations."* Believing in Muhammad's prophecy, I decided to dedicate my life to 'Jihad' or 'Holy War' as the means to obtain either victory or martyrdom. In Islam, martyrdom constitutes the only way a Muslim can guarantee salvation and entrance into heaven. The Qur'an states:

"And reckon not those who are killed in Allah's way as dead; nay, they

are alive (and) are provided sustenance from their Lord" (Surah 3:168).

During school riots against what we called 'the Israeli occupation', I would prepare speeches, shout slogans and write anti-Israeli graffiti, all in an effort to provoke students into throwing rocks at the armed Israeli soldiers. We shouted, *"No peace or negotiations with the enemy! Our blood and our souls we sacrifice to Arafat! Our blood and our souls we sacrifice to Palestine - death to the Zionists!"* I vowed to fight my Jewish enemy, believing I was doing God's will on earth. I remained true to my word, participating in riots in schools, on the streets, and even on the holy Temple mount site in Jerusalem, called by Arabs Al-Masjid Al-Aqsa. All through High School I stayed at the forefront of the riot instigators.

Nothing could change my heart. I embodied the typical extreme Muslim fundamentalist ready to die for Islam. I would even pose with a sad face for my School picture, as if I knew that my martyrdom could come at any moment. I often risked being killed during youth protests and clashes with the Israeli Army, as I threw rocks and Molotov cocktails fighting in the Palestinian Intifada or 'uprising'. Of course, to die fighting the Jews would ease Allah's anger towards my sin, but I possessed no certainty that my good deeds would outweigh my bad deeds on judgment day. How I longed to secure a good spot in heaven with beautiful wide-eyed women to fulfil my most intimate desires!

Once, in a Bethlehem theatre, I watched a film called *21 Days in Munich*. The moment we saw the Palestinians throwing grenades into the helicopter killing the Israeli athletes, hundreds of viewers clapped and yelled *"Allahu akbar!"* (Allah is great). During our Islamic studies in Bethlehem High School we asked our lecturer if Muslims could rape Jewish women after a victory at war. He responded, *"The women captured in battle have no choice in the matter, they are concubines and they need to obey their masters. Having sex with slave captives is not a matter of choice for them."* As it is written in the Qur'an:

"Forbidden to you are...all married women, except those taken prisoners in war: (this) is Allah's ordinance to you" (Surah 4:23-4).

That Muhammad married 14 wives including several slave girls from his victorious battles presented no problem to us. In another passage the Qur'an says:

"O prophet; we have made lawful to thee thy wives whom thou hast given their dowries, and those whom thy right hand possesses out of those whom Allah has given to thee as prisoners of war" (Surah 33:50).

In an attempt to change the hearts of Palestinians, Israeli TV would show World War II Holocaust documentaries. The policy failed. I sat eating my meals, watching and cheering the Germans. Once our School took us for a week to a Jewish camp on the coast of Eshdod, to encourage us to mingle with other Jewish schools. That failed too. We mocked every teacher who spoke to a Jew.

My mother, on the other hand, tried to teach me what she called 'God's plan'. She spoke to me about Bible prophecy; she said that the return of the Jews to Palestine fulfilled the foretold plan of God. She viewed this as a miracle in our generation for the world to see that *"His will shall be done."* She also told me about many future events prophesied in the Bible, but nothing she said had any effect on me. My heart remained set exclusively on fighting the Jews. My mother, under the influence of an American Missionary couple, secretly underwent baptism after she became a Christian.

Due to frequent trips to museums in Israel with my mother, I fell in love with archaeology. It fascinated me. In my many arguments with my mother I would bluntly tell her that the Jews and Christians stood guilty of corrupting the Bible. She responded by taking me to the Scroll Museum in Jerusalem and showing me the scroll of Isaiah, still intact. This 2,000 year old manuscript agrees with the one still used by Christians and Jews today. I could not answer this challenge. However, I still tormented my poor mother by calling her an 'infidel' and a 'damned American imperialist' who claimed that Jesus was the Son of God. I showed her the pictures in the newspaper of all the teenagers 'martyred' as a result of Israeli violence, demanding that she answer. I hated her and begged my father to divorce her and remarry a good Muslim woman.

I lived in Israel throughout the Six Day War, the PLO resistance, the Jordanian black September civil war, the bloody wars in Lebanon and the war of Yom Kippur. Despite all the loss of life on the Palestinian side, we still hoped for that one victory that would rid us of Israel forever. Finally, I ended up being thrown in prison by the Israeli Army. My mother went to the American Council in Jerusalem to try to have me released. She became so anxious and worried that her hair began falling out. Meanwhile, in prison, I learned so much more about the art of terrorism that, upon my release, I became more fanatical than ever.

When I graduated from high school, my parents sent me to the United States for higher education. I immediately involved myself with many anti-Israeli social and political events. My favourite joke at the time? *"Do you know why I hate Hitler? Because he didn't finish the job."* With Hitler as my idol, and Muhammad as my prophet, I pursued my life with scant regard for anyone except fellow Muslims. I believed that one day the whole world would submit to Islam - if not through peaceful means, then by war. With one billion Muslims in the world, I believed that it could happen. Although living far away in America, thoughts of the thousands of Muslims who had died in the last 20 years in countries like Syria, Jordan and Lebanon, lingered freshly in my mind. Thoughts of revenge consumed me.

However, despite the harsh, angry, violent exterior, underneath I nursed a constant fear of the repeated and frequent threats of hell fire for this sin and that, contained throughout the Qur'an. I longed to reach out to my Maker and say, *"I am sorry, please forgive me and give me another chance."* I always wondered about my destiny. I felt sure that, at the end, my sins would heavily outweigh my good deeds. All I could see before me was a life full of sin and having to face death 'hoping the best' that I would find the love and mercy of my Maker at the end.

Sometime in 1992, I read a fascinating book entitled *Armageddon, Appointment with Destiny* by Grant Jeffrey. He explained many detailed Biblical prophecies about Jesus: his birth, life, death and resurrection and the re-creation of the state of Israel. All of the prophecies, written before the birth of Jesus, came to pass just as the Bible predicted! Jeffrey explained the tremendous odds against so many detailed prophecies actually coming true. I could not refute his reasonings and eventually came to the firm conclusion that the Bible must have had a divine origin - God Almighty.

Then the struggle began. The more discovered, the more puzzled I became. How could the Bible be false, corrupted by the Jews, if the very land in which I grew up represented a veritable archaeological 'book', with every dig only further confirming the truth of the Bible? I just had to read the Bible for myself, to discover the true identity of Jesus Christ. I started reading what Jesus claimed for Himself. I found, for example, that Jesus said:

"I am the Alpha and the Omega, the Beginning and the End, says the Lord, who is and who was and who is to come, the Almighty" (Revelation 1:8).

Jesus Christ also said (to the Jews):

"Truly, truly I say to you; before Abraham existed I AM [God]*"* (John 8:58).

These statements reminded me of amazingly similar claims made by Muslims for Muhammad. We believed him to be the intercessor for us on the day of judgment and the world's last and final prophet and saviour. If Muhammad's claims were true, then who was Jesus? That question troubled me a good deal. Jesus and Muhammad might both be wrong. But one thing was certain – both could not be right. Was either of them the true Redeemer and Intercessor for mankind? Vowing to make a decision for 'the truth', I stayed up late, night after night, examining the Qur'an and the Bible, comparing notes. At some point during my study, I prayed: *"God, you are the Creator of heaven and earth, the God of Abraham, Moses, and Jacob, you are the beginning and the end, you are the truth, the only truth, the Maker of the true Scripture, the one and only word of God. I suffer to find your truth, I want to do your will in my life, I long for your love and in the name of the truth I ask. Amen."*

I wanted real gold and had no desire to settle for a cheap imitation. One factor constantly gave me faith to believe in the Qur'an. I knew that it contained modern scientific facts, written a thousand years before their discovery. Did the Bible contain such things too? I spent a month, using a computer program, searching for scientific facts in the Bible. I found that all the scientific facts in the Qur'an, and many more, were already in the Bible hundreds, in some cases thousands, of years before the Qur'an saw the light of day – such as the fact that the earth is round (Isaiah 40:22); hangs on nothing (Job 26:7); has a water cycle (Ecclesiastes 1:7) and mountains at the bottom of its seas (Jonah 2:6), to name but a few.

However, when I compared the stories in the Qur'an with the Bible and archaeology, I found it had many serious errors. My belief in the 'miraculous' Qur'an began to crumble. I felt the sinking sand under me. Through my study of the Bible, I confirmed that hundreds of detailed and unique prophecies had been fulfilled to the letter. Since God is the only one who holds the key to the future and only the Bible reveals the future - not the Qur'an - I knew at that moment that I would be a fool to know all of this and continue worshipping anyone else than the God of the Bible. When I prayed that prayer about truth, I really thought that God would lead me to the Qur'an, but that did not transpire. God says in the Bible:

"For I am God, and there is no other; I am God and there is none like Me, declaring the end from the beginning, and from ancient times things that are not yet done, saying: My counsel shall stand, and I will do all My pleasure" (Isaiah 46:9-10).

Why had I never been exposed to this kind of evidence before? With the help of the Bible, the blindness fell away from my eyes. I came to view sin as the source of all man's problems and the Devil as man's worst enemy (not the Jews!). I saw my need of salvation. The word 'truth' stuck in my heart day and night. I learned that Jesus, the man from my hometown, was a Jew and that my hometown, 'Beth-Lechem', means 'house of bread'. Jesus said:

"I am the Bread of Life, he who comes to me shall never hunger, and he who believes in me shall never thirst" (John 6:35).

10

Jesus came from the enemy of my people - the Jews. Yet, He died for my sin! I had never heard of an enemy who died for another enemy and loved him so much that he allowed Himself to be beaten, spat on, mocked and finally crucified. Long before his death on the cross Jesus said:

"Love your enemies, bless those who curse you, do good to those who hate you, and pray for those who spitefully use you and persecute you" (Matthew 5:44).

Christ, a man of supreme love, practised what He preached. The truth was in front of my very eyes - Jesus Christ is the truth! I called on Him to save me and He answered. I was blind and sought the truth, and now I see. I was bound but now I am free! Christ said:

"I am The Way, The Truth and The Life, no one comes to the Father except through Me" (John 14:6) and *"If the Son* [the Lord Jesus] *therefore shall make you free, you shall be free indeed"* (John 8:36).

My way of thinking, my feelings and my goals in life changed from that point in time. Thank God for real repentance. Then, amazingly, I began to feel for the Jewish people. All the hatred left me. The desire to see them hurt vanished. Instead of laughing at images of the Holocaust on TV, I weep. Knowledge of the truth was a blessed transfer for me. From believing in Hitler to believing in Christ; from believing lies to knowing the truth; from being spiritually sick to being healed; from living in darkness to seeing the light; from hate to love and from evil works to God's grace through Christ. I have repented and accepted the risen Christ as my Lord and Saviour; to Him I have submitted. Jesus said: *"Come to me all you who labour and are heavy laden, and I will give you rest"* (Matthew 11:28).

The Persecuted Professor

by
Dr. M. A. Gabriel*
Former Professor of Islamic history
at Al-Azhar University, Cairo, Egypt

The Al-Azhar University in Cairo, Egypt, from which I graduated, is the oldest and most prestigious Islamic University in the world. It serves as the spiritual authority for Islam worldwide. I taught there during the week and performed the duties of an Imam at the weekend at a Mosque in the city of Giza, Egypt (where the pyramids are located). Among other responsibilities, I used to preach each Friday from noon to 1pm.

One particular Friday my topic concerned 'Jihad'. I told the two hundred fifty people seated on the ground before me: *"Jihad is defending Islam against the attacks of the enemies. Islam is a religion of peace and will only fight against one who fights it. These infidels, heathens, perverts, Christians and Allah's grievers, the Jews, out of envy of peaceful Islam and its prophet, spread the myth that Islam is promulgated by the sword and violence. These infidels, the accusers of Islam, do not acknowledge Allah's words."* At this point I quoted from the Qur'an: *"And do not kill anyone whom Allah has forbidden, except for a just cause"* (Surah 17:33). I preached my sermon on Jihad that day in accordance with the philosophy of the Egyptian government. Al-Azhar University focused us on 'politically correct Islam' and purposely overlooked areas of Islamic teaching that conflicted with its own expedient interpretation.

Outwardly I preached what they taught me, but inside, confusion reigned. I knew that to keep my position at Al-Azhar, I needed to keep my thoughts to myself, only too aware of what happened to people who differed from Al-Azhar's agenda. A dismissal would have rendered me 'unfit' to teach at *any* University in the nation. Yet I knew that my sermons on Jihad at the Mosque and at Al-Azhar conflicted with the Qur'an, all of which I had memorized by the age of twelve. How could I preach about an Islam of love and forgiveness, while Muslim fundamentalists - the ones claiming to be practising true Islam - were regularly bombing churches and killing Christians?

After an upbringing in a well-established Muslim family, in adulthood I studied Islamic history in depth. Although not personally involved in anything radical, one of my Muslim friends, a chemistry student, belonged to an Islamic group active in slaughtering Christians. One day I asked him, *"Why are you killing our neighbours and countrymen with whom we grew up."* He was angry and astonished at my challenge. *"Out of all Muslims you should know. The Christians do not accept the call of Islam, and they are not willing to pay us the jizyah* [tax] *to have the right to practise their beliefs. Therefore, the only option they have is the sword of Islamic law."*

My conversations with him drove me to pore over the Qur'an and the books of Islamic law, hoping to find something to contradict what he said. I soon realized I had two basic options. I could continue to embrace a 'Christianized' form of Islam - an Islam of peace, love, forgiveness and compassion, tailor-made to fit the Egyptian government, politics and culture - thereby keeping my job and status; or I could become a member of the Islamic movement and embrace the Islam of the Qur'an, based on the teachings of Muhammad.

I had tried to rationalize the kind of Islam to which I held. After all, there are verses in the Qur'an about love, peace, forgiveness and compassion. Conveniently ignoring the parts about Jihad, I sought out interpretations of the Qur'an which would not advocate the killing of non-Muslims, yet I kept finding support of the practice. Islamic scholars agreed that Muslims should enforce Jihad on infidels (those who reject Islam) and renegades (those who leave Islam). These contradictions in the Qur'an presented a real stumbling block to my faith.

I spent four years earning my Bachelor's degree, graduating second out of a class of 6,000. Then another four years for my Master's and three more for my Doctorate - all in Islamic studies. That's why I knew the contradictions in the Qur'an so well. In one place alcohol was forbidden; in another it was allowed (compare Surah 5:90–91 with Surah 47:15). In one place it says Christians are good people who love and worship one God (Surah 2:62, 3:113–114). Then you find other verses that say Christians must convert, pay tax or be killed by the sword (Surah 9:29-30). In one place man is said to have been made from water (Surah 21:30); in another he comes from a blood clot (Surah 96:1-2); in yet another from dust (Surah 3:58). Certainly the scholars had theological 'solutions' to these problems, but I wondered how Allah, almighty and all powerful, could either contradict himself or at least change his mind so much. Even the prophet of Islam, Muhammad, practised his faith in ways that contradicted the Qur'an. The Qur'an said that Muhammad was sent to show the mercy of God to the world. But he became a military dictator, attacking, killing and taking plunder to finance his empire. Then, again, Islam is full of discrimination - against women, against non-Muslims, against Christians and most especially against Jews. Hatred is built in to the religion. The history of Islam, which was my special area of study, could only be described as a river of blood.

Inevitably I reached the point where I questioned Islam and the Qur'an with my students at the University. Some of them, members of terrorist movements, were enraged: "*You can't accuse Islam. What has happened to you? You should be teaching us. You must agree with Islam.*" The university heard about it, and I was called in for a meeting in December 1991. I told them what was in my heart: "*I can no longer say that the Qur'an comes directly from heaven or from Allah. It cannot be the revelation of the true God.*" To them it was nothing short of blasphemy. They spat in my face. One man cursed me; "*You blasphemer. You bastard.*" The University fired me and called the Egyptian secret police.

My whole family lived together in a three-storey house - my parents, my four married brothers with their families, my unmarried brother and myself. Only my married sister lived elsewhere. The house was divided into several comfortable apartments, with my brother and I sharing the ground floor with our parents. At three o'clock in the morning the next day, my father heard knocking at the door of our house. When he opened the door, fifteen to twenty men rushed in carrying assault weapons. They were not wearing uniforms. They ran all through the house, waking people up looking for me. Trapped, I had no time to run. My family was terrified. They wept as I was dragged away. Everybody in the area heard the commotion.

Later that morning my parents frantically tried to figure out what had happened to me. They went to the Police Station and demanded, *"Where is our son?"* But nobody knew anything about me. The Egyptian secret Police saw to that. They put me in a cell with two radical Muslims accused of committing terrorist acts. One, a Palestinian, the other, an Egyptian. For three days I was denied food and water. The Egyptian constantly asked me, *"Why are you here?"* I refused to answer, afraid he would kill me if he knew that I harboured questions about Islam. On the third day, I told him I taught at Al-Azhar University and held the position of an Imam in Giza. Immediately he gave me a plastic bottle of water and some falafel and pita that were brought to him by his own visitors, despite the Police warning him not to give me anything. On the fourth day, the interrogation began, the goal of which seemed to be to make me confess my rebellion against Islam.

My interrogator sat behind a large desk. Behind me were two or three police officers. He felt sure that my conversion to Christianity involved someone else. *"What pastor did you talk to?"* he demanded. *"What church have you been visiting? Why have you betrayed Islam?"* The questions seemed endless. On one question I hesitated too long before answering. My interrogator nodded to the men behind me. They grabbed my hand and held it down on the desk. My interrogator took a lit cigarette, reached over and extinguished it into the top of my hand. The scar is there to this day. So is the scar on my lip, where I received the same treatment. The pressure increased with time. One officer pressed a red-hot poker into the flesh of my left arm. They wanted me to

15

confess that I had been converted, but I said, *"I didn't betray Islam. I just said what I believe. I am an academic person. I am a thinker. I have a right to discuss any subject of Islam. This is part of my job and part of any academic life. I could not even dream of converting from Islam - it is my blood, my culture, my language, my family, my life. But if you accuse me of converting from Islam for what I say to you, then take me out of Islam. I don't mind being out of Islam."*

My answer didn't please them. I was taken to a room containing a steel bed. They tied my feet to the foot of the bed and then put heavy stockings on them. An officer with a four foot long whip began lashing my feet. I was beaten unconscious. When I woke up the officer stopped and untied me. *"Stand up,"* he demanded. I could not at first, but he beat my back until I complied with his request. He pointed down a long passageway. *"Run,"* he bellowed. Again, when I could not do it, he whipped my back until I ran down the passageway. When I reached the end, there was another officer waiting for me. He whipped me until I ran back. They made me run back and forth repeatedly. Then I was put in a tank full of ice-cold water. I have low blood sugar, so it wasn't very long before I passed out again. When I awoke I was lying on the steel bed, still in my wet clothes.

Further tortures followed. One evening I was taken behind the building. I saw what looked like a small, concrete room with no windows or doors. The only opening was a skylight in the roof. They made me climb a ladder to the top. *"Get in,"* they ordered. When I sat on the edge and put my feet down in the opening, I felt water. I could also see something swimming on the top of the water. *"This is it"*, I said to myself, *"this is where I will die."* I slid down into the opening and felt the water rise up my body, but then to my surprise I felt solid ground under my feet. The water came up to my shoulders. Rats started crawling over my head and face. They closed the skylight. Terrified, I remained there all night. The next morning when the skylight opened, hope revived that I might survive.

The interrogation continued. The officers took me to the door of a small room and said, *"There is someone in there who loves you very much and wants to meet you."* I was hoping it might be a family member or a friend. They opened the door. Inside I saw nothing but a large dog. The door shut behind me. I cried out from my heart to my Creator, "*You are my father, my God. Please look after me. Can you leave me in these evil hands? I don't know what these people are trying to do to me, but I know you will be with me and one day I will see you and meet you.*" I walked to the middle of the room and slowly sat down cross-legged on the floor. The dog came and sat down in front of me. Then it started circling me, as if preparing to eat me. To my relief it simply sat down and stayed by my side. I was so exhausted I fell asleep. When I woke up, the dog was in the corner of the room. When the officers finally opened the door they saw me praying, with the dog sitting next to me. I heard one say, "*I can't believe this man is a human being. This man is a devil - he's Satan.*"

"*I don't believe that,*" the other replied, "*There is an unseen power standing behind this man and protecting him.*"

The first officer concluded; "*What power? This man is an infidel. It's got to be Satan because this man is against Allah.*"

In my absence, my Egyptian cellmate asked the police, "*Why are you persecuting this man?*" They told him, "*Because he is denying Islam.*" He was furious. When I rejoined him in the cell, he was ready to kill me. But I had only been in there twenty minutes when a police officer came with transfer papers for him and he was taken away. "*What is going on here?*" I thought to myself, "*What power is protecting me?*" At that time, I did not know the answer. Shortly thereafter my own transfer papers came through. My destiny? A permanent prison in southern Cairo. All of this for merely 'questioning' Islam. My faith was really shaken.

My first week in Cairo was relatively relaxed. Thankfully my prison guard did not agree with radical Islam. Throughout this whole time my family persisted in trying to find out my whereabouts. They had no success until my mother's brother, who was a high-ranking member of the Egyptian Parliament, returned to the country from travelling overseas. My mother called him, sobbing, "*For two weeks we have not known where our son is. He is gone.*" My uncle had the necessary connections. Fifteen days after I was kidnapped, he came to the prison personally with release papers and took me home.

Later, the police gave a report to my father: "*We have received a fax from Al-Azhar University accusing your son of leaving Islam, but after an interrogation of fifteen days, we found no evidence to support it.*" My father was relieved to hear this. I was the only one in the family who had studied Islam at the University, and he was very proud of me. That I would ever leave Islam was, to my father, unimaginable. He attributed the whole incident to jealousy. "*We don't need them,*" he said, and then asked me to start work immediately as a sales director in his successful clothing manufacturing business.

For the following year I lived in a vacuum. I had no faith, no God to pray to, to call on, to live for. I believed in the existence of a God who was merciful and righteous, but I had no idea who He was. Was He the God of the Muslims, the Christians or the Jews? Or was He some animal - like the cow of the Hindus? I had no idea how to find Him. If a Muslim concludes that Islam is not the truth, where can he turn? Faith is in the fabric of the life of a Middle Eastern person. He cannot imagine life without God. The events of the year took their toll. I was constantly tired and suffered continually from headaches. I began visiting a nearby pharmacy one or two times a week to buy a packet of tablets. After a while, the pharmacist asked me, "*What is going on in your life?*"

"*Nothing is going on,*" I answered. "*I have no complaint except for one thing: I am living without God. I don't know who God is, who created me and the universe.*"

Startled, she said, "*But you were a professor at the most respected Islamic University in Egypt. Your family is very respected in the community.*"

"*That is true,*" I replied, "*but I have discovered falsehoods in their teachings. I no longer believe my home and family are built on a foundation of truth. I had always clothed myself in the lies of Islam. Now I feel naked. How can I fill the emptiness in my heart? Please help me.*"

18

"OK." she said. *"Today I will give you these tablets, and I will give you this book - the Bible. But please promise me not to take any tablets before you read something from this book."*

I took the book home and opened it at random. My eyes fell on Matthew 5:38: *"You have heard that it was said, An eye for an eye, and a tooth for a tooth, but I tell you not to resist an evil person. But whoever slaps you on your right cheek, turn the other to Him also."* My whole body began trembling. I had studied the Qur'an my whole life - not once had I found anything like this. I had come face to face with the Lord Jesus Christ.

As I continued to read I lost all track of time. It felt as if I was sitting on a cloud above a hill, and in front of me was the greatest teacher in the Universe revealing all the secrets of heaven to me. Compared to what I had learned from my years of studying the Qur'an, there was no doubt in my mind that here, in the Bible, I was finally encountering the true God. I was still reading into the early hours of the next day, and by dawn I had repented and accepted the Lord Jesus Christ as my Saviour, believing that He died for my sins and rose again from the dead. The only people I told were the Pharmacist and his wife. In Egypt, if anyone leaves Islam, it is automatically assumed that he has become a Christian and therefore must be killed.

Somehow the news leaked out. The fundamentalists sent two men to ambush and kill me. While returning home on foot from a social visit to a friend's house about a twenty minute walk away in Giza, I was on Tersae Street, near my home, when I saw two men standing in front of a grocery shop. Dressed traditionally in white robes, long beards and head coverings, I thought they must be customers. However, as I reached the shop they stopped me and pulled out knives with which to stab me. I put up my hands to protect myself. Again and again the blades struck me, cutting my wrists. The other people in the street gathered to watch, but no one helped me. The first attacker was trying to stab my heart. He missed and penetrated my shoulder instead. When he pulled the knife out I fell to the ground in a little ball, trying to protect myself. The other attacker tried to stab me in the stomach, but the blade turned, and he stabbed me in the shin instead. I passed out. Apparently two police officers arrived on motorcycles and my attackers ran away. I was taken to the hospital and treated. Again, my father rejected any thought that I was abandoning Islam. He just could not think in those terms.

I continued to work for my father, not speaking of my new faith. In fact, he sent me to South Africa in 1994 to explore business opportunities for him. While there, I spent three days with a Christian family from India. When we parted, they gave me a small cross on a necklace to wear. This small cross marked the turning point in my life. After a little more than a week back home, my father noticed it. *"Why do you wear this chain?"* he demanded.

"Father, this is not a chain," I explained. *"This is a cross. It represents Jesus, who died on a cross like this for me, for you and for everybody in the whole world. I have received Jesus as my God and Saviour, and I pray for you and for the rest of my family to also repent and accept Jesus Christ as your Lord and Saviour."*

My father collapsed in the street. Some of my brothers rushed out and brought him into the house. My mother started crying in fear. I stayed with them as they bathed my father's face with water. When he came to, he was so upset he could hardly speak, but he pointed at me. In a voice hoarse with rage he cried out, *"Your brother is a convert. I must kill him today!"* Wherever he went, my father carried a gun under his arm on a leather strap. He pulled out his gun and pointed it at me. I started running down the street and, as I dived around a corner, I heard the bullets. I ran for my life to my sister's house about half a mile away. I asked her to help me get my passport, clothes and other documents from my father's house. She wanted to know what was wrong, and I told her, *"Father wants to kill me."* She asked why. I said, *"I don't know. You must ask Father."*

When I ran away, my father knew exactly where I was headed because my sister and I were very close. He walked to her house, arriving while we were talking. He banged on the door. He was openly sobbing with tears streaming down his face, *"My daughter, please open the door."* Then he shouted, *"Your brother is a convert! He has left the Islamic faith. I must kill him now!"*

My sister opened the door and tried to calm him down. *"Father, he is not here. Maybe he went to another place. Why don't you go home and relax, and later we can talk about this as a family."*

My sister had mercy on me and gathered my things from my parents' house. She and my mother gave me some money. I left on the evening of August 28, 1994. For three months I struggled through Northern Egypt, Libya, Chad and Cameroon. I finally stopped in the Congo where I contracted malaria. I found an Egyptian doctor to examine me. He said that I would be dead by morning and made arrangements to get a coffin from Congo's Egyptian embassy to send me back home. To their shock, I survived the night. I left the hospital after five days.

Ten years have gone by since I was saved from my sins and received peace with God through the Lord Jesus Christ. He called me and gave me a personal relationship with Him - something that Islam never offered. There is a statement about God in the Bible which is unique. It says *"For God so loved the world, that He gave His only begotten Son, that whoever believes in Him, should not perish, but have everlasting life"* (John 3:16). In Islam you must love Allah in order for Allah to love you in return. Surah 3:30 states *"If you love God...God will love you."* In the Bible however, God loves sinners first in order to secure their salvation. *"We* [believers in Jesus] *love Him because He first loved us"* (I John 4:19). *"But God demonstrates His own love toward us, in that while we were still sinners, Christ died for us"* (Rom 5:8). May my life story help you to appreciate and accept this unique love and grace.

---

* Dr. Gabriel is not the Professor's birth name. After four years of persecution in South Africa, subsequent to his conversion to Christ, he decided to change his name for security reasons. He chose the name 'Mark' because tradition says that the early disciple of Christ called Mark, who wrote one of the four gospels, was the first person to bring the gospel to Egypt after the resurrection of Jesus.

A Loyal Son of Islam

by
Rezi Sabri
from Iran

With mounting anticipation, I waited for just the right moment to launch a revenge attack against the enemy of my people and my God. From my hiding place I intently eyed two approaching Armenians. "*How filthy and unfit as human beings they are,*" I thought to myself. As the men came closer I pondered the best course of action whereby to inflict injury and pain. I watched as they descended the steep hill directly across the street from me. I could see the face of the paralysed Armenian Christian who was sitting motionless in his wheelchair. He was young, perhaps in his early twenties. The man who was pushing him stopped in front of a house. He carefully set the brakes to prevent the chair from rolling forward and then entered the house.

Suddenly I realised the time had come for the assault. With a shout of triumph I sprang from the alley and ran furiously across the street. My enemy looked up at me. Though but for a moment, time seemed to stand still as our eyes met. Burning with hatred, I glared into the man's terror-filled face. He began begging, crying, and screaming not to be hurt. But my heart was hardened against him, in determination to fulfil my plan. Grasping the wheelchair, I gave it a hard shove. It began moving down the hill, rolling faster and faster until it crashed into a wall. The wheelchair overturned, hurtling the young cripple to the ground where he lay sobbing, unable to lift himself up.

At the sound of his screams, the paralysed man's companion rushed out. A small crowd quickly gathered. Further anger stirred within me as I watched the group of sympathizers. My rage and hatred boiled over. I began hurling rocks and insults upon them all. They turned to stare at me as if I were insane. I was alone but felt quite safe. No one in the Christian ghetto dared to apprehend me. I had fulfilled my duty in despising these followers of Christ. I felt no regret for my actions. The feeling of dominance was exhilarating. As I returned home to my mother, I smiled as I thought of how I had successfully demonstrated loyalty to my Muslim faith.

My attitude and actions were not unusual for an average 12-year-old child in Iran. Christians were outcasts in our Muslim community and we were taught to hate them. Harassing followers of Christ presented a favourite pastime for us young ones. We delighted to abuse, insult, mock and attack them - and their church buildings. Whoever was most successful in tormenting them was hailed by his peers as worthy of the highest respect and praise.

Born in 1936, the youngest of six children of prosperous parents in Rezahe, Abidajan, in Iran, my father ran a successful construction business and my mother was from an affluent and notable family. While only six years old my father died, but my mother raised her children with great ability, which included ensuring her children imbibed her Shi'ite faith. There are several distinct sects of the Muslim religion in Iran, and each one holds to beliefs that contradict the others. Although the Shi'a sect worldwide numbers significantly less than the major Sunni sect, approximately eighty five to ninety percent of Iranians are Shi'ites.

The Shi'a Muslims believe in Allah 'the Most High God', and Muhammad, his prophet or 'Messenger from God'. Allah hears our prayers and is merciful and forgiving. If one believes in him and follows his instructions in righteousness, he will find mercy, the forgiveness of sins and the eternal reward of heaven. Yet the main motivation for allegiance to Allah is neither love nor the development of a relationship with him. It is considered presumption and ignorance to entertain the notion that one can actually know the living God. For me, as a Muslim, fear of Allah's wrath compelled me to submit to his will. The word 'Islam' means 'submission'. Shi'ites are dedicated to following the teachings of the twelve Imam (leaders), who held political influence and interpreted Muhammad's teachings through the centuries. To become a Muslim and attain heaven, one must believe there is one God and that Muhammad is his Prophet. Believers in Islam must make the confession of faith, called a 'witness': "*I believe that there is no god but God, and that Muhammad is the Prophet of God.*" This statement is more than a testimony of what one believes; it is really an oath or a pledge to follow the Islamic way of life.

Pilgrimages to tombs constitute an important part of religious tradition in Shi'a society. During these pilgrimages money is offered in sacrifices at various tombs and shrines, as the Shiites pray to the dead. Asking for forgiveness, they kiss the tombs of Shi'a saints, placing written prayers on them. Dead Imams are honoured so highly that prayers are offered to them in the hope of receiving an answer. I participated in these activities, often spending time weeping at the tomb of my father. Reciting repetitious prayers which had little meaning to me, I prayed for my father to forgive me and for him to be forgiven by merciful Allah.

In 1969, I came to America where I eventually married, had a son, and became owner and chef of a restaurant in Denton, Texas. Sadly, my wife and I divorced and I had the responsibility of single-handedly bringing up my son. Up until 1973, I had never had a spiritual conversation with a Christian. In Iran it was considered a sin to eat with one or to visit one in his home. If it was unavoidable, one had to wash one's hands three times to cleanse oneself of a Christian handshake, or shower three times to cleanse oneself of the contamination of a Christian home.

One night, as I slept, I dreamt that I was leafing through the pages of a notebook. The pages seemed to become alive. They were transformed into a living person who was larger than a mountain. When I saw his face, terror filled me. I was sure he was going to harm me. Fire flashed from his eyes. The heat in his eyes was attracting me but I could not approach him. As I beheld the brilliance and beauty of his countenance my fear subsided. No human language could explain or define such a scene of glory as I saw in that vivid dream.

Five years later, in 1979, I related the dream to my neighbour, Merv Waage. Merv was a lawyer and a dedicated Christian. I told him how the dream had always intrigued me. Did it have a meaning? Merv told me that my answer was in the Bible. Taken aback I laughed loudly. I did not want to even look at a Bible, never mind read it! Muslims call the Bible the 'Injil' (the Gospel). It belongs to Jesus Christ, or 'Isa Massih' as we call him: Jesus the Messiah. It is a book pertaining only to Christians. Could I possibly find the meaning of my dream in such an unclean book?

Regardless, Merv marked the references in the Bible that he felt described my dream and gave me the Bible. I took the Bible to my office at the restaurant. At first I feared that if I opened the Bible I might go to hell. However, I took the challenge and read the passages in the book of Daniel, chapter ten, and in Revelation, chapter one - the places marked for me by Merv. After reading these verses four or five times I stood to my feet and said loudly, "*It is Him! What the Bible describes is all I saw!*" I believed the person I had seen was Jesus Christ in His glory, as others who had seen Him described him. I closed the Bible and began weeping. I could not explain my feelings. A great calm and stillness came over me. All the sounds and voices in the restaurant around me seemed to be miles away, as the reality of this revelation hit home. Still in shock, I wiped the tears away from my eyes and walked out of my office. As one of my employees passed by, I turned around, grabbed him and asked him, "*Do you believe in Christ?*" This employee was a fellow Muslim. I urgently repeated the question again. The employee replied, "*Yes, we respect the prophets.*" At this answer, I began shaking him and said, "*No! No! Do you believe in the Christ?*" The employee answered, "*Yes, we believe that he lived.*"

My mind reeled from the conflict between everything I had been taught to believe, versus this apparent eternal truth. I left my dazed employee in the restaurant and took a drive in my car. I continued to weep periodically for the rest of the day while still being filled with a deep peace. Although God had invaded my life in such an extraordinary way, in the long term I remained unchanged for the most part. I was mentally conscious that God had touched me and that I had 'seen' Jesus Christ, but I still did not believe in Him. I somehow pushed aside the memory of that day. From time to time it returned to haunt me. How could I forget the beauty of Christ? My friend Merv thought I had become a believer and I was happy for him to believe that - but it wasn't true.

After years of persistent pleading, Merv finally managed to persuade me to attend a church meeting. The preacher invited me to tell the congregation of my vision. I decided to pretend that I was a Christian. The fateful Sunday in October 1983 arrived. All of these people were expecting me to talk about their leader whom I did not know! I told them that my life had totally changed and a list of other things I knew they wanted to hear me say. I told them that I believed that Jesus was my Saviour, but it was all lies.

That night at bedtime, my distress banished any sleep I had hoped for. Thoughts of hatred, loneliness, helplessness and even death filled my mind. I did not even retire to bed, but instead lay on the floor. In my distress I finally cried out in my native Persian tongue, *"God!"* At that moment a fear of hell came before my mind. I had never fully believed in hell up to that moment. *"What is He going to do to me now? What an evil person I am."* I realised I was a lost sinner, helpless to save myself and dependent entirely on Christ, His death and resurrection, for my sins to be forgiven. I cried out to heaven from the depths of my soul, *"Forgive me, God!"*

When I awoke the following morning, I knew a peace greater than I had experienced when I first read about Christ in the Bible. As I spoke with my son, Alex, that morning, he asked me, *"Daddy, what's the matter with you? You're so quiet. You look calm. You're not screaming or impatient or mad at me."* It was as if a light turned on in my mind. *"Jesus did it,"* I said.

Alex asked, *"How?"*

"I asked Him," I replied.

Alex responded, *"Why didn't you ask Him before?"*

"I didn't know Him before," was all I could say.

Soon the magnitude of the effect of my conversion dawned upon me. I knew that this was not just a 'social change' brought about by my own will. I was a different person. I knew I had been born again but I was unsure of how to relate to Christians in light of my Muslim upbringing. I had much to learn. At first I struggled to balance my cultural heritage with my new spiritual life. However, as I immersed myself in the Bible and submitted to the Lordship of Christ daily all doubt and uncertainty left me. Joy flooded my heart.

As of 2003, I am 67 years old. I have come a long way from the time and place when I hated all Christians. My chief desire for the future lies in pursuing the spiritual goals that the Lord Jesus has set out for me in His word. I know that nothing can happen to me unless God allows it. The time may come when I will be martyred for Christ. But for the Christian there is no more death. In a sense, I have already died and entered into a spiritual union with the Lord Jesus. He lives forever, never to die again, and He has become my life. The Lord Jesus said that in order for a person to enter God's kingdom he must be born again. In other words, he must die to his old life and let the Spirit of God give him a new life - spiritual life (John 3:3). He also said, *"I am the way, the truth and the life. No man comes to the Father but through me"* (John 14:6). Only Jesus Christ can give freedom from the power of Satan.

I learned from the Bible that all men are dead in their sins and are enemies of God, but that Jesus Christ came to earth, not to make bad people good, but to make dead people live. Sincerity alone cannot gain us acceptance with God. One can practice religious customs in all seriousness and with true dedication, while all the time being spiritually dead. Religion without Christ is meaningless (Romans 6:23, John 10:10). Jesus said that we must repent of our sins (confess our guilt and turn from sin with our whole heart) and believe in Him for salvation. He also said that if any man would follow Him he must deny himself and take up his cross. To a true Christian, following Christ's teachings and doing His will become more important than anything else. His Spirit gives us love for all men and enables us to speak the truth to others who do not know Him. Jesus said that if we confess Him as Lord before men He would not be ashamed to confess us before His Father in heaven (Luke 12:8, Mark 8: 38).

My prayer is that you will come to know the peace and joy that I have found in having the guilt of my sin removed by the mercy and forgiveness of God through the Lord Jesus Christ. Salvation for an individual is not given at the subjective whim of Allah. It is based on the just payment for sin by Jesus Christ on the cross. In Islam sin is not paid for, it is weighed on a balance scale. However, in the Bible we read: *"There is one God and one Mediator between God and men, the Man Christ Jesus, who gave Himself a ransom for all"* (I Tim 2:5-6). Jesus was more than just a messenger from God. Much, much more. On the cross Jesus became the sacrifice for sin. He paid a debt He did not owe, because we owe a debt of sin that we could not pay for in a million years of good works. Good works cannot cancel sin. The Bible states quite clearly that we are all born in sin:

"Behold, I was brought forth in iniquity, and in sin my mother conceived me" (Psalm 51:5).

Furthermore, we are helpless to save ourselves:

"For by grace you have been saved through faith, and that not of yourselves; it is the gift of God, not of works, lest anyone should boast" (Eph 2:8).

But the wonderful truth is that through turning from sin and believing in Christ we can receive the free gift of everlasting life:

"For the wages of sin are death, but the gift of God is eternal life in Christ Jesus our Lord" (Rom 6:23). May it be so in your experience too.

I Dared To Call Him Father

by
Bilquis Sheikh
from Pakistan

Born in 1920 into a family of noble birth, Bilquis Sheikh, as a middle-aged married woman was deserted by her husband, a general and a minister in the Pakistani government. She retreated to her family mansion to live out her life in tranquil luxury with her grandson and fourteen servants. It was here that some extraordinary things began to happen.

"La illaha illa Allah, Muhammad rasul Allah (there is no God but Allah and Muhammad is the prophet of Allah)."

The call drifted through her bedroom window. Every morning for 46 years it had echoed in her ears. The normalcy of the call to prayer was a comfort after the strangeness of the previous night, when Bilquis had experienced an evil presence in her garden. Being a practical woman, she had tried to rationalise away the experience, but when her grandson also experienced a similar presence, she took the advice of her maids and summoned the local Mullah. For three days he recited prayers and portions of the Qur'an in Arabic. Everything seemed to return to normal. In her biography Bilquis relates the story:

"After these experiences I found myself drawn to the Qur'an. Perhaps it would help to explain the events and at the same time fill the emptiness within me. Certainly its curved Arabic script had often sustained my family in the past. Previously, I had read the Qur'an as a duty. This time I felt I should really search its pages. I took my copy, which had belonged to my mother, relaxed on the white eiderdown coverlet of my bed and began to read. I started with the very first revelation to the young prophet Muhammad, as he sat by himself in a cave on Mount Hira:

'Read in the name of thy Lord who created, He created man from a clot. Read and thy Lord is most honourable, who taught [to write] *with the pen, taught man what he knew not'* (Surah 96:1-5).

"At first I was lost in the beauty of the words. But later on in the book there were words that did not comfort me at all:

'And when you divorce women and they reach their prescribed time, then either retain them in good fellowship or set them free with liberality' (Surah 2:231).

"My husband's eyes looked like black steel when he told me that he did not love me anymore. I shrivelled inside as he spoke. What had happened to all our years together! Could they be dismissed just like that? Had I, as the Qur'an said, 'reached my term'? The next morning I picked up the Qur'an again, hoping to find the assurance I needed so desperately. But the assurance never came. I found only directives on how to live and warnings against other beliefs. There were verses about the prophet Jesus whose message, the Qur'an said, had been falsified by early Christians. Though born of a virgin, Jesus was not God's son. *'Say not three'*, warns the Qur'an against the Christian concept of the Trinity. *'Desist, it is better for you. God is only One God: far be it from His glory that He should have a son'* (Surah 2:171).

"Back in my bedroom that evening as I read, the Qur'an's many references to the Jewish and Christian writings, which preceded it, again impressed me. Perhaps, I wondered, I should continue my search among those earlier books? But that would mean reading the Bible. How could the Bible help since, as everyone knew, the early Christians had falsified so much of it? But the idea of reading the Bible became more and more persistent. But where would I obtain a Bible? Perhaps Raisham (my maidservant) would have a copy. But I dismissed the thought. Even if she did, my request would frighten her. Pakistanis have been murdered for even appearing to persuade Muslims to turn traitor-Christian.

"I could understand why Raisham, a Christian, refused to talk about the murder of a Muslim who had recently become a Christian. She knew, as well as I did, who had killed that girl. The girl had forsaken her Muslim faith to be baptised a Christian. So her brother, infuriated by the shame this sin had brought upon his family, had obeyed the ancient law of the faithful, that those who fall away from their faith must be slain."

In the end Bilquis asked her Christian chauffeur to procure a Bible for her. He was so afraid that Bilquis had to threaten to fire him before a Bible mysteriously appeared on a table. When her daughter, Tooni, called in to see her, she noticed the Bible on the table and asked Bilquis to read something from it.

"Light-heartedly, I opened the little Bible and looked down at the pages. Then, a mysterious thing happened. It was as if my attention was being drawn to a verse in the lower right hand corner of the right page. I bent close to read it:

'I will call them My people, who were not My people; and her beloved, who was not beloved. And it shall come to pass in the place where it was said to them, You are not my people; there they shall be called the sons of the living God' (Romans 9:25-26).

"I caught my breath and a tremor passed through me. Why was this verse affecting me so? I closed the book, murmured something about this not being a game anymore and turned the conversation to another subject. But the words burned in my heart. Early in the evening of the next day, I retired to my bedchamber where I planned to rest and meditate. I took the Bible with me and once again leafed through its pages. I read another puzzling passage:

'But Israel, pursuing the law of righteousness, has not attained to the

law of righteousness' (Romans 9:31).

"Ah, I thought, just as the Qur'an said; the Jews had missed the mark. The writer of these passages might have been a Muslim, for he continued to speak of the people of Israel as not knowing God's righteousness. But the next passage made me catch my breath again. *'For Christ is the end of the struggle for righteousness by the law to everyone who believes'* (Romans 10:4). I lowered the book down for a moment. Christ? Was He the end of the struggle? I continued to read: *'For the word is near you, in your mouth and in your heart...that if you confess with your mouth that Jesus Christ is the Lord, and believe in your heart that God has raised him from the dead, you will be saved'* (Romans 10:8-9).

"I put the book down again, shaking my head. This directly contradicted the Qur'an. Muslims knew the prophet Jesus was only human, that he did not die on the cross but was whisked up to heaven by God and a look-alike put on the cross instead. Now dwelling in an inferior heaven, this Jesus will someday return to earth to reign for forty years, marry, have children, and then die. In fact, I heard that there is a special grave plot kept vacant for his remains in Medina, the city where Muhammad is also buried. On the day of resurrection, Jesus will rise and stand with other men to be judged before Almighty God. But this Bible said Christ was raised from the dead. It was either blasphemy or...my mind whirled. I knew that whoever called upon the name of Allah would be saved. But to believe that Jesus Christ is God? Even Muhammad, the final and greatest of the messengers of God, the Seal of the Prophets, was only mortal.

"I lay back on my bed, my hand over my eyes. If the Bible and Qur'an represent the same God, why is there so much confusion and contradiction? I do not know when I fell asleep."

After further study and some vivid dreams, Bilquis, armed with many questions, decided to visit some educated Christians. That evening she drove her black Mercedes to the home of the Mitchells. His shocked wife opened the door, only to see Bilquis standing there. She came to the point quickly. She asked Mrs. Mitchell whether she knew anything about God. Mrs. Mitchell's answer startled Bilquis: *"I'm afraid I don't know too much about God,"* she said, *"but I do know Him."*

"Mrs. Mitchell," Bilquis gasped, *"forget I am a Muslim. Just tell me: what do you mean when you say you know God?"*

"I know Jesus," replied the preacher's wife. Bilquis relates what happened next. "Then she told me what God had done for her and for the world, by breaking the dreadful deadlock between sinful man and Himself by personally visiting this earth in human flesh (the Lord Jesus Christ) and dying for sinners on the cross. The room was quiet again. I could hear trucks passing on the nearby main road. Mrs. Mitchell seemed in no hurry to speak. Finally, hardly believing my own ears, I took a deep breath: *'Mrs. Mitchell, some peculiar things have been happening at our house lately. Events of the spirit. Good and bad; both. I feel as if I am in the midst of an immense tug of war and I need all the help I can get. Could you pray for me?'*

"The woman appeared startled at my request, then, collecting herself, she asked if I wanted to stand up, kneel or sit down as we prayed. I shrugged, suddenly horrified. All were equally unthinkable. But there was this slender, youthful woman kneeling on the floor of her bungalow. And I followed her! *'Oh Spirit of God,'* said Mrs. Mitchell in a soft voice, *'I know nothing that will convince Begum Sheikh who Jesus is. But I thank You that You take the veil off our eyes and reveal Jesus to our hearts. Oh, Holy Spirit, do this for Begum Sheikh. Amen'.*"

Bilquis returned home and read John's Gospel, as Mrs. Mitchell had recommended her to do. She immediately read a startling announcement about Jesus, *"Behold, the Lamb of God who takes away the sin of the world"* (John 1:29). Some days later, Bilquis had to take her grandson into hospital. In the waiting room she read her Bible, which caught the eye of a Christian doctor. After a discussion, the doctor, with tears in her eyes, encouraged Bilquis to pray to God in a personal way.

"Why don't you pray to the God you are searching for?" she said. *"Ask Him to show you His way. Talk to Him as if He were your friend. Talk to Him as if He were your Father."*

"On returning home I prayed, '*I am confused, Father. I have to get one thing straight right away.*' I reached over to the bedside table where I kept the Bible and the Qur'an side by side. I picked up both books and lifted them, one in each hand. '*Which, Father?*' I asked. '*Which one is your book?*' The thought came to me - in which book is God revealed as a Father? Why, the Bible of course!'"

There and then a battle began to rage as Bilquis determined to read the New Testament right the way through. She now fully realised she would have to accept Jesus as the Son of God to know the forgiveness of her sins and eternal life in Heaven. She thought of all the rejection she would receive from her family. 'Traitor' – that's what they would call her. Fear came over her as she recalled the Islamic command that '*Whoever of you turns back from his religion, then he dies while an unbeliever, these...are the inmates of the fire* [hell]' (Surah 2:217). But the Lord Jesus Christ, in the Bible, demanded total allegiance and would not settle for anything less than complete submission and commitment. As she came to Revelation, the last book of the Bible, she read:

"*See, I stand knocking at the door. If anyone listens to my voice and opens the door, I will go into his house and dine with him, and he with Me*" (Revelation 3:20).

Bilquis saw the issue clearly. The scriptures, the dreams, the intervention of Christians - everything was conspiring to point her in one direction. Decision time loomed. Accept or reject? Open the door or close it. She knelt in front of the fire. From her broken, repentant and divinely convinced heart, she cried out in faith, '*Oh God, don't wait a moment. Please come into my life. Every bit of me is open to You.*' She believed on the Lord Jesus Christ. She was saved and she knew it. It was 3 O'clock in the morning on December 24th, 1966.

What a change came over Bilquis! She was a new person in Christ. As time passed, she invited all the poor people from the village into her mansion. Instead of looking down on the poor, she embraced them. Instead of being a bitter recluse who constantly scolded her servants, she became gracious and joyful. With Christ's help she could forgive her husband for dumping her. She discovered that when she lived in obedience to Christ, a wonderful peace and presence of God was with her; but when she disobeyed, by acting in pride or self-sufficiency, she felt God's presence withdrawing. In this way, and as she studied the Bible, she discovered how to live a consistent Christian life.

Word leaked out that she had become a Christian and that she attended a Christian group. Her family rejected her as a traitor. The local people abused her. Threatening letters and telephone calls started coming her way. Most of her servants fled as rumours increased that some religious Muslims from the Mosque were plotting her death after Friday prayers. The threat of being burnt out was very real. One day she smelt smoke. Thankfully, Bilquis and her servants managed to extinguish the flames before the whole house caught fire. Finally in 1972, after experiencing 6 years of persecution, Bilquis and her grandson left for America where she lived until 1997. At the age of 77 she passed into the wonderful presence of her beloved Saviour to be with Him forever.

I Was A Mullah

by
Rehmat Ullah
from Pakistan

At Rehmat's birth his mother held her head high; she had given birth to a male child. He was born into a family of Pathans - a faithful and devout Islamic people who would prefer to die rather than to betray their faith and tradition. Rehmat was given to Allah's service while still a child and was later sent to Madrasa, a Qur'anic school. By the time he was eight he had read the whole of the Qur'an and, by the age of fifteen, he knew it by heart in Arabic. Yet he did not understand what it meant because his native tongue was Pushtu. *"The Qur'an is learnt by heart in Arabic, the holy language of Allah"*, says Rehmat. *"Becoming a 'Hafiz' (reciter) of the Qur'an is highly valued in my culture. There is a belief among some Muslims, including my family, that if a man learns the Qur'an by heart, seven generations of that man are pardoned by Allah."*

Rehmat furthered his studies of the Qur'an and the Hadith at the esteemed Jama Ashrafia Institution in Lahore, Pakistan, and after completing his studies was appointed an Imam (Muslim priest) in Bahawalpur, Pakistan. His reputation soon spread. People from nearby villages started coming to him for 'Tawizes' (charms).

"In many ways life seemed all right, yet at the same time I felt a sort of emptiness and all my ritual prayers and chanting of the Qur'an gave me no satisfaction. There was something missing," recalls Rehmat.

Then the unthinkable happened. He began to question some of the fundamentals of the Islamic faith. For instance, how can a man please his Maker by doing good works? Rehmat had a strong feeling that he would never be able to do enough good to balance out his sins. Even his role as a Mullah seemed insufficient to satisfy God.

"The Tawizes I wrote for innocent people are such a deception, that only one who is involved in that business would know what I am talking about. I knew I was deceiving God and people", says Rehmat.

One day, conversing with a stranger while waiting for a train, he discovered the man was a follower of Jesus. He was reading the Bible. Questions flew back and forth as the discussion developed into a fierce argument. It became so involved that they agreed to miss the train, go inside and continue their conversation in the restaurant. When the food came, the man asked Rehmat if he minded a blessing being said for the food.

"During his prayer he really prayed from his heart and said, 'Lord, please help all those who are in any kind of need, regardless of their clan or creed'. This prayer stunned me, as a Muslim. What a difference! I used to curse those who followed Jesus and here was this man who blessed even his enemies."

When they parted, the stranger gave Rehmat his Bible. Back at home he read it for hours, but the differences between the Bible and the Qur'an confused him. He thought much upon deep spiritual matters daily. During this period of mental conflict, Rehmat travelled abroad to visit some of the holy places of Islam. Sadly, he returned to his country feeling as empty as when he had left. Totally disillusioned he tragically concluded that God did not even exist. He gave up his Imam's post, which he had held for 18 years - and he stopped praying.

His renunciation of God brought him no peace either! Emptiness and despair dogged his footsteps. Finally Rehmat locked himself in his room, taking the Bible and the Qur'an with him. He felt he should give God another chance. *"I am neither a Muslim nor a follower of Jesus, but I believe there is only one true God,"* Rehmat prayed. *"If you are really there, then please show me the right path or else take back the breath you have given me."*

He read both books in earnest. He read, wept and prayed. After some time he fell asleep and began to dream. In fact he had several vivid dreams about matters of life and death and the person of Christ over the next 48 hours. When he awoke he kneeled down and for the first time in his life he prayed in the name of Jesus. He now earnestly desired a new life in Christ.

He went to see a Christian preacher who loved the Lord Jesus and asked for his help. The preacher explained to him more about the gospel of Christ. Through repentance towards God and trusting in the Lord Jesus Christ who died on the cross for his sins, Rehmat had his guilt removed. He believed in his heart that Christ the Lord rose again from the dead. He was saved! Rehmat received the righteousness of God that guarantees access to His eternal presence. He did not earn this free gift by his own goodness or charitable deeds; he freely received it from the risen Christ. Rehmat is clear about the change that Christ has performed in him and he has an assurance of eternal salvation and the forgiveness of his sins that he never found in Islam, even as a Mullah.

Soon he was baptised and given a new name, Rehmat Paul. *"When I arrived back home, the news of my baptism had already reached my family. When they asked me about it and I would not deny my faith, I was severely beaten by my family members. I was thrown out and rejected. Life sometimes seems painful, but I am not worried about the loss for I have peace with God and I know what my destiny is."*

The Bible says, "Who shall separate us from the love of Christ? Shall trouble or hardship or persecution or famine or nakedness or danger or sword? No, in all these things we are more than conquerors through him who loved us" (Romans 8:35-37).

To the Reader

The Hajj, or Pilgrimage, forms one of the five pillars of Islam and constitutes the trip of a lifetime to any Muslim who can afford it! Its customs are fascinating. For instance, at Mecca all Muslims must wear special white robes called 'Ihram', before they can enter the holy place where the Ka'aba (the Black Rock) resides. A symbol of purity, many Muslims believe that by wearing these robes they become pure and are granted eternal life.

While there are always pickpockets and thieves among the crowd at the Ka'aba, for which reason guards are placed on duty, most pilgrims strongly desire to be found pure and acceptable before a holy, pure and perfect God. But no matter how hard we try to keep God's holy law, we fall short. We sin outwardly because we are sinners inwardly. No washing with water or wearing of white robes can remove this problem. We may sincerely hope that, on the day of judgment, our good deeds will outweigh our bad deeds and that God will have mercy on us and let us into Heaven rather than send us to Hell – after all, Allah is merciful! But is this a hope based on truth – or is it just wishful thinking?

Muhammad was well aware of his own sins. In the Hadith (Islam's second most holy book after the Qur'an) he said: *"O Allah, set me apart from my sins, as the East and the West are set apart from each other, and clean me from sins as a white garment is cleansed of dirt. O Allah! Wash off my sins with water, snow and hail"* (Hadith Vol. 1, No. 711). *"By Allah! I ask for forgiveness from Allah and turn to him in repentance more than seventy times a day"* (Hadith Vol. 8, No. 319). Muhammad had no assurance of going to Heaven when he died because he was not sure whether his good deeds would outweigh his bad deeds. He remarked: *"By Allah, though I am the Apostle of Allah, yet I do not know what Allah will do to me"* (Hadith Vol. 5, No. 266).

If Muhammad wasn't sure of heaven, what hope is there for us? None. The Bible reveals the impossibility of attaining God's perfect standard and therefore a place in heaven when it states: *"For there is no difference* [between all types of people in the world] *for all have sinned and fallen short of the glory of God"* (Romans 3:23). Even our good deeds have no merit before God in our sinful condition. The Bible says: *"For all of us have become like one who is unclean, and all our righteous deeds are like a filthy garment"* (Isaiah 64:6). Allah may be merciful - but on what basis? If by 'mercy' we mean that Allah will simply overlook, ignore and then swap our good deeds against our bad deeds, that makes Allah a compromiser – not a God to be trusted or believed in.

There is one exception to the universal plague of sin. According to the Qur'an Jesus (Isa) was perfect. Quoting the angel Gabriel (Jibra'il), the Qur'an says of Mary's son Jesus: *"I am only a bringer of a message from thy Lord, that I will give thee a pure boy"* (Surah 19:19). Born of a virgin, the Bible also states clearly that Jesus was without sin: *"In Him is no sin"* (I John 3:5).

Thus, only through Christ can we receive the true spiritual Ihram (white robes), that will shield us from God's judgment. The Bible says: *"For He has clothed me with garments of salvation, He has wrapped me with a robe of righteousness"* (Isaiah 61:10). We need God's righteousness - not our own.

Eid Al Adha

Another Hajj custom is the 'Eid Al Adha' (feast of sacrifice). In memory of Abraham offering up his son to God, pilgrims at Mecca bring a lamb for ritual sacrifice, part of which they eat, before giving away the rest as a gift to the poor. There is an important spiritual application here. The Qur'an says: *"And We* [God] *ransomed him* [Abraham's son] *with a great sacrifice"* (Surah 37:107). Now, in the Bible, the Jews used to sacrifice animals to God as an atonement for their sins - but these sacrifices could not actually remove sin; they were meant only to point forward to a final and complete sacrifice in the future. The Bible declares: *"And every priest stands, ministering daily and offering repeatedly the same sacrifices, which can never take away sins. But this man* [Jesus]*, after he had offered one sacrifice for sins for ever, sat down at the right hand of God"* (Hebrews 10:11-12). The sacrifices pointed forward to the sacrificial death of Christ.

40

Ka'aba

The Ka'aba is the focal point of the Hajj and, indeed, of all Islam. Here it all began. It is 'most holy ground'. Pilgrims press forward through the huge crowds in order to touch or kiss the Rock. By this act many believe they will be healed or have their sins taken away.

But this Rock, after all, is only a rock – not God. Our sins do indeed need to be forgiven - but rock kissing can never accomplish the purging of sins. It is Jesus the Messiah who atones for sin. Ironically Jesus is called in the Bible, *"a chief corner stone...and he that believes on him shall not be put to shame"* (I Peter 2:6).

Abb-a-Zamzam

Pilgrims also visit a place where Muslim tradition says God opened a spring of water for Hagar and Ishmael. There they buy holy water that has healing properties and can purify one whoa person who drinks it. Water is only water, but this custom does signify the longing of the pilgrims to find God. Jesus Christ knows that men and women are thirsty for true satisfaction. He stated: *"Everyone who drinks of this water* [from the well in Samaria] *shall thirst again, but whoever drinks of the water that I shall give Him shall never thirst...If any man is thirsty, let him come to Me and drink. He who believes in Me, as the Scripture has said, out of his heart will flow rivers of living water. But this He spoke concerning the Spirit, whom those believing in Him would receive"* (John 4:13-14, 7:37-38).

Only through the Lord Jesus Christ can sinners come to know God in a real and personal way. Christ offers a relationship, not a religion. To those who repent of their sins against God and put their trust alone in the Lord Jesus for salvation, God will give His Holy Spirit, as well as giving them an assurance of a place in heaven. Amazing – salvation, forgiveness, eternal life, a home in heaven - all through turning from sin and believing in the Lord Jesus Christ as the Son of God who loved you and gave Himself for you on the cross, rising from the dead the third day. Yet, there are many obstacles to faith.

Obstacles In The Way Of Faith

Obstacle One: Has The Bible Been Changed?

Unlike many of today's Muslims, Muhammad never accused Christians of changing the Bible. In fact Muhammad held the Bible in high esteem. God told him, *"We [Allah] revealed the Torah [first 5 books of the Bible]"* (Surah 5:44). Muhammad was also told: *"If thou [Muhammad] art in doubt as to what We [Allah] have revealed unto thee, ask those who read the book before thee; the truth has indeed come to thee from thy Lord"* (Surah 10:94). *"We revealed the Torah [the first five books of the Bible] in which was guidance and light...they [the Jews] were required to guard the book of God and they were witnesses thereof ...whoever does not judge by what God revealed, these are the unbelievers...And we sent after them in their footsteps Jesus, the son of Mary, verifying what was before him in the Torah"* (Surah 5:44-47). Jesus stamped His seal of approval on the Bible. He said: *"Thy Word is truth"* (John 17:17).

Yes, the Qur'an accuses the Jews of distorting the word with their tongues (Surah 4:46), of perverting its meaning (Surah 2:75), of inventing their own Scriptures to sell for profit (Surah 2:79) and still others of concealing the truth (Surah 2:146). But never does the Qur'an accuse the actual Bible text of being corrupt. In fact, Muhammad gives this severe warning to anybody who rejects the Bible: *"Those who reject the Book and that with which We sent Our apostles...when the fetters and the chains shall be on their necks; they shall be dragged into hot water; then in the Fire shall they be burned..."* (Surah 40:70-72).

Muslims who say that the Bible has been changed and that they cannot therefore accept the crucifixion, resurrection and Deity of Christ, are often not aware of the hundreds of ancient hand-written Bible manuscripts in various languages (Hebrew, Syriac, Latin etc.) that predate Muhammad by centuries. Examples of these are the Codex Vaticanus (AD 325-50), which contains virtually the entire Bible and the Codex Sinaiticus (AD 350) which contains nearly all of the New Testament (Injil) and over half of the Old Testament. Apart from this there are Injils from earlier periods such as the Bodmer Papyrus 11 (AD

150-200) and the Chester Beatty Papyri (AD 200). Since the discovery in Israel of the Dead Sea Scrolls (dated at between 200 BC and AD 68), experts have agreed that the standard of accuracy exhibited by the Jewish scribes, who transcribed the Biblical texts, is without parallel in ancient history.

But this is not all. Early Christian leaders like Justin Martyr and Chrysostom quoted extensively from the Injil. From the two hundred year period just after the deaths of the apostles of Jesus (100-300 AD), over 36,000 quotations from the Injil still exist – in the writings of the 'early church fathers'. Scholars state that, even if every Bible in the world was destroyed, the entire Injil could be reconstructed from the quotations in these writings of the early church fathers alone, with the exception of just eleven verses! So, it is a certain fact of history that the Bible is a reliable and trustworthy book. Sir. Frederic Kenyon (former principle, head librarian and world manuscript expert of the British museum) has written:

"The Christian can take the whole Bible in his hand and say without fear or hesitation that he holds in it the true Word of God, handed down without essential loss from generation to generation throughout the centuries" (Our Bible and the Ancient Manuscripts, p.23, New York: Harper and Brothers, 1941).

Islamic scholars, such as Muhammad Ata ur-Rahim and Ahmad Deedat, claim the existence of an original Injil that was lost for over 1,000 years, but was rediscovered during the Middle Ages. This 'Gospel of Barnabus' agrees with Muslim beliefs and they claim it is therefore the true Injil. There are multiple facts that disprove this theory. The Gospel of Barnabus was actually written *after AD 1300* (700 years after Muhammad) for the following reasons:

1. The writer mentions the year of jubilee *"which now cometh every hundred years"* (Barnabus 82). The jubilee to which he refers was not decreed until AD 1300, by Pope Boniface VIII.
2. He also quotes from Dante's 'Divine Comedy', which was not written until the 14th century (Barnabus 23, 135, 178).
3. He says 1st Century Israel used a 'feudal system', something that

belonged to the Europe of the Middle Ages (Barnabus 194) and that 1st Century Jews stored wine in wooden casks – rather than in wineskins (Barnabus 152).

4. The author reports a 1st Century three-cornered war involving 600,000 Jews. Each 'corner' had 200,000 soldiers (Barnabus 91). This is a historical impossibility. The Jews, living under Roman occupation, were hard pressed to find any weapons at all, never mind 600,000 swords! Besides this, such a force, if united, was twice the size of the entire Roman army at that time!

The conclusion of genuine scholarship is that the 'Gospel of Barnabus' was written sometime after AD 1300 by a Spanish speaking Muslim and, as such, represents a forgery.

But what of the contradictions in the Bible? By checking with other scriptures, reading the context and noting the historical period and culture, all of these so-called contradictions can easily be cleared up. For example, Numbers 25:9 states that 24,000 people died in a plague. However, in the New Testament, Paul says that 23,000 of them died in one day (1 Corinthians 10:8). Is there a contradiction? No, clearly 23,000 died *in one day*, the rest dying later. In John 6, Jesus miraculously feeds a crowd of 5,000 with five loaves of bread and two fish. In Mark 8, Jesus feeds 4,000 with seven loaves and a few small fish. Contradiction? No. Jesus himself refers to both events as being on separate occasions (Mark 8:17-20).

Obstacle Two: Did Jesus Die On The Cross?

In the Qur'an it says: "*And their* [the Jews] *saying: We have killed the Messiah, Jesus, son of Mary, the apostle of God; and they did not kill him nor did they crucify him, but he was made to resemble (one crucified), and those who differ therein are only in a doubt about it; they have no knowledge respecting it, but only follow a conjecture, and they killed him not for sure*" (Surah 4:157).

However, another Qur'anic verse has Jesus saying: "*And peace on me on the day I was born, and on the day I die, and on the day I am raised to life*" (Surah 19:33). Did Jesus die and rise again, according to the

Qur'an? Islamic scholars hotly debate this point. Surah 3:54 states: *"When God said, O Jesus! I will cause thee to die and exalt thee in my presence...then to Me shall be your return."*

The Qur'an seems to tell us that Christ died and then was taken up to Heaven. Ibn Hamid says: *"God caused Isa, Son of Mary, to die three hours and then raised Him"* (Jamia al bayan 3:289-292). Muhammad Ibn Ishaq reckoned that Jesus was dead for seven hours before God raised Him to Heaven. Al Rabia Ibn Uns on the other hand, thought that Jesus died and was taken immediately to Heaven. Perhaps we ought to take Muhammad's advice in the Qur'an when confronted by such confusion and go to the Bible for answers (Surah 10:94)! In the Bible, the crucifixion and death of Jesus was continually predicted long before He was even born.

David (1,000 BC) quoting Christ prophetically says: *"You [God] have brought me to the dust of death...they pierced my hands and my feet"* (Psalm 22:15-16).

Isaiah (700 BC) said: *"But He was wounded for our transgressions...He poured out His soul unto death"* (Isaiah 53:5, 12).

The Injil itself makes it abundantly clear that Jesus *did* die on the cross, rise from the dead and later ascend back to heaven. It also records the fact that Jesus repeatedly predicted these very events e.g. Luke 18:31-33. As further written proof there is the testimony of 1st century eyewitnesses such as:

Matthew the Tax collector: *"They...crucified Him...and Jesus yielded up his spirit"* (Matthew 27:35, 50)
John the fisherman: *"The soldiers...crucified Jesus...and bowing his head, he gave up his spirit"* (John 19:23, 30)
Peter, another fisherman: *"Who Himself bore our sins in His own body on the tree [cross]...For Christ also died for sins once for all, the just for the unjust, in order that He might bring us to God, having been put to death in the flesh, but made alive in the spirit"* (I Peter 2:24, 3:18).

It is this death and resurrection of Jesus Christ that Christians have been celebrating for 2000 years! When Christians take the bread and the cup each Sunday throughout the world, they are proclaiming the death of Christ until He returns. When they baptise believers in water they are proclaiming Christ's death and resurrection.

In a court of law, when the enemies and friends of the accused person testify to the same thing, it is taken as true. Among Jesus' strongest opponents were the Jews. Most of them did not accept Him as Messiah and the Son of God, but all accepted the fact that He was killed by crucifixion. The Jewish Talmud says: *"On the eve of Passover they hanged Yeshu (of Nazareth)...they found naught in his defence and hanged him on the eve of Passover"* (Babylonia Sanhedrin 43a). 'Yeshu' is the Hebrew word for Jesus.

Josephus, a Jewish historian, wrote: *"Now there was about this time [about AD 30] Jesus, a wise man...He was the Christ; and when Pilate, at the suggestion of the principal men amongst us, had him condemned to the cross, those that loved him at the first did not forsake him, for he appeared to them alive again the third day..."* (Antiquities 18:3:3).

The Roman historian, Tacitus, wrote: *"Christus, the founder of the name, was put to death by Pontius Pilate, procurator of Judea in the reign of Tiberius..."* (Annals 15:44). Other ancient historians, such as Lucian of Samosata, Mara Bar-Serapion, Thallus and Phlegon, all speak of the crucifixion of Christ. The fact is, to deny the death and resurrection of Christ compares with denying that Muhammad ever went to Mecca!

Obstacle Three: Is Jesus the Son of God?

Muhammad asked *"How could He [God] have a son when He has no consort?"* (Surah 6:102). Furthermore, Surah 9:30 states: *"...the Christians say: The Messiah is the Son of God. These are the words of their mouths; they imitate the saying of those who disbelieved before; may God curse them!"* Here Muhammad compares what Christians believe with the ideas of Pagans (the unbelievers before them). However, Pagans believed in many 'sons of god' produced by a deity like Zeus, an idea mutually offensive to Christians and Muslims.

46

Christians believe that the Bible uses the term 'Son of God' to convey equality and sameness of nature, not subordination and subservience; thus the need for a 'consort' is irrelevant.

The virgin birth is tied directly to the fact that Jesus is God's Son. The Holy Spirit (not Gabriel) came upon Mary so that, when she supernaturally conceived, the child's Father was not Joseph (Luke 1v35). That is why Christians call Jesus the Son of God, or God the Son. Interestingly, the Qur'an recounts an angelic promise made to Mary about a child called Jesus. Mary responded, *"My Lord! How shall there be a son (born) to me, and a man has not touched me?"* (Surah 3:46), thus confirming the virgin birth contained in the Bible hundreds of years before.

While many prophets conveyed God's message or word, none except Jesus received the title 'God's Word' (Surah 4:171). What does this mean? When in doubt about these things we need to look at the Bible, just as Muhammad said. In the Injil there is a very revealing passage: *"In the beginning was the Word, and the Word was with God, and the Word was God. He was in the beginning with God. All things were made through Him, and without Him nothing was made that was made...And the Word became flesh and dwelt among us, and we beheld His glory, the glory as of the only begotten of the Father, full of grace and truth...No one has seen God at any time. The only begotten Son, who is in the bosom of the Father, He has declared Him"* (John 1:1-18).

Did Jesus ever claim to be the Son of God? According to the Injil He clearly did. In the Jews' religious court, Jesus was asked by the High Priest, *"Tell us if You are the Christ, the Son of God!"* Jesus answered, *"It is as you said,"* (Matthew 26:63-64). He had already clearly stated earlier, *"I am the Son of God"* (John 10:36). For this 'blasphemy' the Jews wanted to kill Jesus. They said *"You, being a man, make yourself out to be God"* (John 10:33). This formed the charge at Jesus' trial. Pilate, the Roman judge, was told, *"He ought to die, because He made Himself the Son of God"* (John 19:7). Not only did Jesus' disciples believe Him to be the Son of God and worship Him as such, but even Pagan Romans, like the Centurion at the crucifixion, exclaimed, *"Truly this was the Son of God!"* (Matthew 27:54).

Obstacle Four: Is There a Trinity?

The Bible reveals one God who exists in a three-dimensional way as Father, Son (or Word) and Holy Spirit – the 'Trinity'. His creation mirrors this in remarkable ways. Time is one, yet has three dimensions: past, present and future. Space is one; but exists as height, depth and width. The Universe is one, yet it exists as time, space and matter. Human beings are one, yet exist as body, soul and spirit (the mathematics of the Trinity is not 1+1+1=3, but 1x1x1=1).

Muhammad refuted what he thought the Christian Trinity meant (Surah 5:73), but in his words he actually speaks against the Pagan idea of 'triads of gods', such as the Egyptian Osiris, his wife Isis, and their son, Horus. This is totally different from the Biblical Trinity. At the time of Muhammad there were heretical Pagan groups in Arabia who mixed some Christianity with their religion. They worshipped God, Jesus, and the goddess Venus, who they turned into the Virgin Mary! *"O Jesus, son of Mary! Did you say to men, Take me and my mother for two gods besides God?"* (Surah 5:116). The Christians were just as horrified about this as Muhammad. Although some so-called churches today pray to Mary and the saints, such a thing is forbidden in the Bible. In the same way, true Muslims should not accept the Shiite practice of praying to the 'saints'.

The first verse of the Bible declares, *"In the beginning God created the heavens and the earth"* (Genesis 1:1). The Hebrew word for God is 'Elohim'. This is a plural word. However, the word 'created' (Hebrew - bara) is in the singular. Thus there is one God who exists in a plural form. Deuteronomy 6:4 states: *"Hear, O Israel: the LORD our God is one LORD"* (Deuteronomy 6:4). The Hebrew word here for 'one' is 'echad', a singular adjectival noun. Yet it follows a plural noun 'God – Elohim'. This is grammatically incorrect, unless God is a 'plural one'. That is why God says in Genesis, *"Let Us make man in Our image..."* (Genesis 1:26).

The fact that God exists distinct from His creation and yet is the 'author of relationships', reveals that He experiences relationship outside of time, space and matter. This is possible because He exists as One God in a plural form. Although the word 'Trinity' is not to be found in the Injil, the truth is found there repeatedly. For example, *"Go therefore and make disciples of all the nations, baptising them in the name of the Father and of the Son and of the Holy Spirit..."* (Matthew 28:18-19. See also II Corinthians 13:14, Titus 3:4-6, Ephesians 2:18 and 3:11-16).

Obstacle Five: Is Muhammad Predicted In The Bible?

The Qur'an claims that Muhammad was predicted in the Bible: *"Those who follow the Apostle-Prophet* [Muhammad], *the Ummi* [the unlettered one], *whom they find written down with them in the Torah and the Gospel..."* (Surah 7:157). What Biblical predictions are thought by Muslims to refer to Muhammad? The first is, *"I will raise up for them a Prophet like you* [Moses] *from among their brethren, and will put My words in His mouth, and He shall speak to them all that I command Him"* (Deut 18:15).

Like unto Moses? Moses was a Hebrew, he came out of Egypt, he spoke to God directly and he performed phenomenal miracles. In what way is Muhammad 'like unto Moses'? Was Muhammad an Israelite? No, he was an Ishmaelite. Did Muhammad come out of Egypt? No, he came from Arabia. Did God speak directly to Muhammad? No, his 'revelations' came through the mediation of the angel Gabriel. Did Muhammad perform any mighty signs and miracles? The Qur'an explicitly says that Muhammad performed no signs (Surah 6:110). We must conclude that Deuteronomy 18:18 cannot refer to Muhammad. So who is the Prophet like Moses? Jesus was an Israelite, that is, of the line of Jacob who was called Israel (Matthew 1:1-16; Genesis 32:28); He came out of Egypt (Matthew 2:13-15); God the Father spoke directly to Him (John 12:28) and He performed mighty miracles (Luke 7:22). The Injil reports: *"Then those men, when they had seen the sign that Jesus did, said, This is truly the Prophet who is to come into the world"* (John 6:14). No wonder the apostle Peter quotes Deuteronomy 18:18 and says that it has been fulfilled in Jesus Christ (Acts 3:18-26).

The second verse is: *"And I will pray the Father, and He will give you another Helper, that He may abide with you forever – the Spirit of truth, whom the world cannot receive, because it neither sees Him nor knows*

Him; but you know Him, for He dwells with you and will be in you" (John 14:16-17). It is claimed by many Muslims that the Christians changed the Greek word 'Perikultos' (meaning 'Praised One', a Greek version of the Arabic 'Ahmad', a root word for Muhammad) into 'Parakletos' (meaning 'Comforter', 'Helper' or 'The One who comes alongside'). However, any knowledgeable scholar in the field will tell you that there is no evidence at all for this 'corruption'. All of the Greek manuscripts in existence, which predate Muhammad, say 'Parakletos', not 'Perikultos'. When we closely examine Jesus' prophecy in John 14:16-17, we notice He prophesied that the Comforter would:

1. Be with the apostles forever
2. Be called the 'Spirit of truth'
3. Be personally known by Jesus' apostles
4. Be inside the apostles.

Now was Muhammad alive at the time of Jesus' apostles? No, he was born nearly 600 years later. Was Muhammad ever called the 'Spirit of Truth'? No. Did Muhammad live with the apostles forever? No. Did Muhammad live inside the apostles? No. It is therefore impossible that Muhammad has fulfilled this prophecy. To whom then does the prophecy apply? The Bible clears the matter up in the following few verses. *"But the Comforter, which is the Holy Spirit, whom the Father will send in my name, he shall teach you all things"* (John 14:26). *"But when the Comforter is come...even the Spirit of truth...He shall testify of me"* (John 15:26). It is certain then, that the Comforter is not Muhammad, but the Holy Spirit of God.

Have you have repented to God and put your faith alone in the Lord Jesus Christ?

If so, you should immediately take the following steps:

1) Thank Him for what He has done for you and ask yourself the question, *"What can I now do for Him?"*

2) Start speaking daily to Him in prayer from your heart, bringing Him praise and thanksgiving, as well as asking Him for blessings.

3) Get a Bible and start reading and studying it. It's best to begin with the Gospels (e.g. Mark or John) and read through the New Testament. Ask God to give you understanding on how to apply it practically to your life.

4) Find a Bible believing Church and attend its meetings every week.

5) Tell others what the Lord has done for you.

If you would like confidential help or further information, please feel free to contact us. We can supply free Bibles, literature and details of Bible believing churches in your area. Our address is:

Penfold Books
P. O. Box 26, Bicester, Oxon, OX26 4GL, England.
Tel: + 44 (0) 1869 249574   Fax: + 44 (0) 1869 244033
E-mail: penfoldbooks@characterlink.net   Web: www.penfoldbooks.com

If this book has been a help to you please let us know.
We greatly value the feedback we receive from our readers.

All quotations from the Qur'an are taken from the translation into English by Maulana Muhammad Ali, who also translated the Qur'an into Urdu.

Acknowledgements:

1. Thanks to Walid for personal permission kindly granted.
2. Used by permission of Mark Gabriel. Abridged from his book *Islam & Terrorism* (Charisma House, Lake Mary, Florida, 2002).
3. Taken from *Reza: A Moslem Sees Christ* by Reza Sabri with Timothy Sheaff. An IMF Publication, P.O. Box 3079, Denton, Texas, 76202, USA.
4. Used by permission of Baker Book House, Grand Rapids, Michigan. From the book *I Dared to Call Him Father* by Bilquis Sheikh with Richard Schneider, Copyright 1978.
5. Thanks to Rehmat Ullah for personal permission kindly granted prior to his recent death. Text taken from *I Was A Mullah*, originally printed in Ye Sach Hai, an Asian Christian magazine. The Light Noor, P.O. Box 587, Dagenham, RM8 2PP.

Recommended websites:

www.answeringislam.org
www.arabicbible.com

Also available:

Dawn of the New Age: *5 New Agers Relate Their Search For The Truth*
Angels of Light: *5 Spiritualists Test The Spirits*
Messiah: *5 Jewish People Make The Greatest Discovery*
They Thought They Were Saved: *5 Born Again Christians Recall A Startling Discovery*

Copyright: Penfold Books 2003

Published by:

Penfold Books
P. O. Box 26, Bicester, Oxon, OX26 4GL.
Tel: + 44 (0) 1869 249574
Fax: + 44 (0) 1869 244033
Email: penfoldbooks@characterlink.net
Web www.penfoldbooks.com

ISBN: 1-900742-12-8